Who Works Here?

Airport

by Lola M. Schaefer

Heinemann Library
Chicago, Illinois

© 2000 Reed Educational & Professional Publishing
Published by Heinemann Library,
an imprint of Reed Educational & Professional Publishing,
100 N. LaSalle, Suite 1010
Chicago, IL 60602
Customer Service 888-454-2279

Printed in Hong Kong
Designed by Made in Chicago Design Associates

04 03 02 01 00
10 9 8 7 6 5 4 3 2 1

Library of Congress Cataloging-in-Publication Data
Schaefer, Lola M., 1950
   Airport / Lola Schaefer.
    p. cm. – (Who works here?)
   Includes bibliographical references and index.
   Summary: Introduces some of the people who work at an airport and
the jobs they perform, including customer service agent, checkpoint
security supervisor, air traffic specialist, flight lineman, and
public safety officer.
   ISBN 1-57572-515-0 (library binding)
   1. Airports   Juvenile literature. 2. Air travel Juvenile
literature.   3. Occupations   Juvenile literature.   [1. Airports.
2. Occupations.]   I. Title. II. Series.
TL725.T39   2000
387.7'364—dc21   99-40767
                                                      CIP

Acknowledgments
All photographs by Phil Martin.

Special thanks to Sandra Lux and the staff at Fort Wayne International Airport in Fort Wayne, Indiana, and to
workers everywhere who take pride in what they do.

Some words are shown in bold, **like this.**
You can find out what they mean by looking in the glossary.

Contents

What Is an Airport?

Every day, millions of people all over the world use airports.

An airport is a place where **aircraft** land and take off. Passengers and cargo arrive and depart on airplanes and jets. Airline company **employees** help passengers with their travel plans and needs.

A terminal is the main building at an airport. Passengers can buy their tickets inside the terminal. People usually get on and off the airplane at a gate in the terminal. Airplanes land and take off on long runways. All the workers at an airport help people and goods travel safely from place to place.

This airport is in Fort Wayne, Indiana. The map shows where all of the people in this book are working. Many airports in the United States look like this.

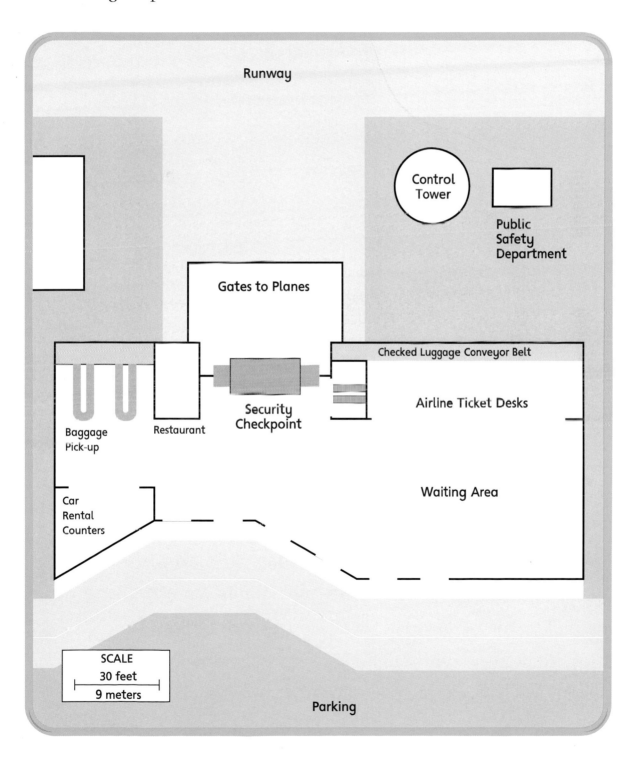

Runway

Control Tower

Public Safety Department

Gates to Planes

Checked Luggage Conveyor Belt

Airline Ticket Desks

Security Checkpoint

Restaurant

Baggage Pick-up

Waiting Area

Car Rental Counters

SCALE
30 feet
9 meters

Parking

Director of the Airport

Skip is the director at this airport. Skip often must work with local government leaders. Here he is signing a letter to the **mayor**.

Most airports have a person who is in charge. This job is often called the director of an airport. The director's job is to oversee all airport operations. The director meets and speaks with the different department managers. He or she must work closely with the city and county **governments**. The director wants the airport to meet the travel needs of the **community**.

Many airport directors, like Skip, have college degrees. Before becoming directors, they worked in airport management for many years. In those years, they learned the skills needed to run an airport safely. After becoming a director, managers can become **certified** airport **executives.** They continue to learn more at meetings each year.

The airport director has many responsibilities. Here, Skip is looking at plans for a new runway that might be built.

Customer Service Agent

Linda is a customer service agent. She announces when flights leave the airport.

A customer **service** agent works for an airline company at the airport. Customer service agents **reserve** airplane flights for passengers and give them their tickets. Then they tag luggage that passengers want to check onto the airplane.

To become a customer service agent, people must go to travel school for several months. They learn how to give customers the best service. They learn what to do if there are ticket problems or weather delays. No matter what happens, a customer service agent should know how to stay calm and helpful.

Linda is also responsible for taking passengers' tickets at the gate before letting them onto the plane.

Customer Service Agents and Jetways

A jetway is an **enclosed** hallway that connects an airplane to the airport. It has large wheels beneath it that help it move forward and backward. When an airplane lands, it parks near a gate and the flight crew opens the front door.

Customer **service** agents are responsible for driving the jetway toward the airplane.

After the jetway connects to the airplane, the flight crew helps passengers **deplane.** If it is raining or snowing, passengers stay dry while walking through the jetway. When the airplane is ready to leave, the customer service agent helps new passengers **board** the plane.

Jetways can go up or down to fit any size airplane.

Checkpoint Security Supervisor

The checkpoint security supervisor works with the staff to keep passengers safe.

Checkpoint security supervisors are responsible for stopping anyone who brings a dangerous item through the checkpoint. In the morning, they test all of the security **equipment.** During the day, checkpoint security supervisors help security workers do their jobs correctly.

All airport visitors pass through the checkpoint on their way to a gate. Visitors must place all bags on a moving belt. A person called a screener looks at the bags as they pass through an X-ray machine.

Suzanne is a screener. She is trained to see any dangerous items in luggage or purses.

PLACE BAGS
LAT ON BELT

Ground Crew

A ground crew **services** the airplane before its next flight. The ground crew is also responsible for guiding the airplane in and out of the gate.

Lita is a customer service agent for an airline company. At some airports, customer service agents help the ground crew by loading luggage into the airplane.

Sometimes the ground crew must melt ice
that forms on the wings of an airplane.

Ground crews train for two weeks on the job. They spend
another six weeks in school. They learn to be alert and
safe while working near the airplane and ground
equipment. The ground crew wears hearing protectors
while working near loud jet engines.

Flight Lineperson

A flight lineperson is careful not to spill any fuel. Spilled fuel can cause explosions and fires.

A flight lineperson is responsible for filling airplane **fuel** tanks. The flight lineperson parks a fuel truck near an airplane at a gate. Then he or she connects a hose from the truck to the airplane to fill the airplane's fuel tank. A flight lineperson can fuel an airplane in ten minutes.

Flight linepersons receive two weeks of on-the-job training. They learn all the safety rules for working with fuel and airplanes. They also learn how to use a tow truck to pull small and large airplanes across the airport.

A flight lineperson must carefully drive a truck that holds about 2,800 gallons (10,640 liters) of fuel.

Flight Crew

Mary, a flight attendant, prepares the snacks and drinks for the passengers.

Flight attendants are part of the flight crew. They greet passengers as they **board** the airplane. Flight attendants speak with the pilots before the airplane takes off to plan a safe and comfortable trip.

Pilots work for an airline company. They are part of the flight crew. A pilot must record a **flight plan** before the airplane leaves the airport. The pilot is in charge of flying the airplane safely to the next airport.

Matt trained for several years to become a pilot. Then he spent eight weeks at airline school learning how to fly this plane.

Air Traffic Specialist

Brady is an air traffic specialist. Brady often talks with his manager about airplane **flight plans.**

An air traffic specialist watches the airfield and **radar** screens to separate **aircraft** and prevent collisions. Air traffic specialists work in the control tower. They also speak with pilots, telling them when to land and take off.

Air traffic specialists work with aircraft within 20 miles (32 kilometers) of the airport. They wear radio headsets to stay in **communication** with the pilots. They speak with the pilots about changes in weather or airport conditions.

Here, Brady uses binoculars to check that the landing gear is down on incoming airplanes.

How Air Traffic Specialists Communicate

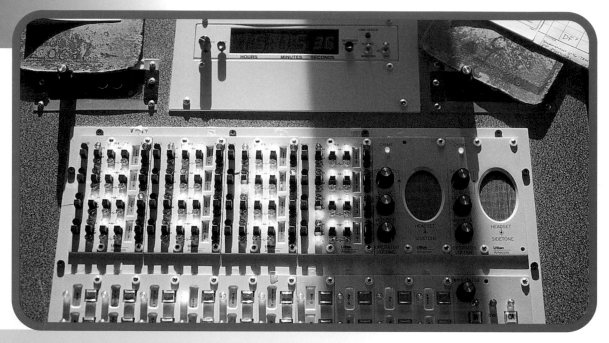

The communications system works 24 hours a day, seven days a week.

Every control tower has a **communications** system. This board of switches and speakers connects the air traffic specialists with air traffic specialists at other airports. Using this system, air traffic specialists can try to help an airplane in trouble.

There is a room in the control tower filled with large **radar** screens. Air traffic specialists watch these screens. They can track and speak with **aircraft** 50 miles (80 kilometers) or more from the airport.

Radar screens help air traffic specialists see the location of aircraft up to 10,000 feet (3,048 meters) high in the sky.

Commander of Public Safety

John is the Commander of the Public Safety Department at this airport. He can speak to the airport or his officers with his patrol car radio.

A commander is in charge of public safety at the airport. The commander and his or her officers respond to all emergency calls from airport **employees**. They are trained to put out **aircraft** fires, rescue people, and stop crimes.

All public safety officers are trained state police officers and firefighters. They continue training each year in law enforcement and emergency medical **services.** The commander chooses the people he or she wants to serve on the team at the airport.

Here, John speaks with an officer before an **equipment** test.

Using Safety Equipment

The top tank on this truck can spray 1,000 gallons (3,785 liters) of water a minute.

Public safety officers use **Aircraft** Rescue Firefighting Vehicles in different emergencies. If there is a fire, this vehicle has two tanks that spray water. Tanks of foam can be used to put out **fuel** fires. **Equipment** called the "jaws-of-life" can remove someone trapped in an accident.

The Aircraft Rescue Firefighting Vehicle has safety features for the officers. All controls can be operated by one person from inside the truck. The windshield is twice as thick as regular windshields, to protect the driver from heat and small flying objects.

DRY CHEMICAL

An officer would use this dry chemical to put out an engine fire.

Car Rental Supervisor

Dawn is a car rental supervisor. She enters a customer's name into the computer to reserve a car.

A car rental supervisor in an airport **reserves** cars and vans for businesspeople and families on vacation. The supervisor works at a counter in the airport terminal. The car rental supervisor rents cars to people who have just arrived on airplanes.

Dawn, like many car rental supervisors, learned her job by working with another car rental person for a month. Supervisors must know all the rules of the car rental company and many ways to help customers. Car rental supervisors like Dawn meet people from all over the world.

Here, Dawn shows a customer the different rental cars.

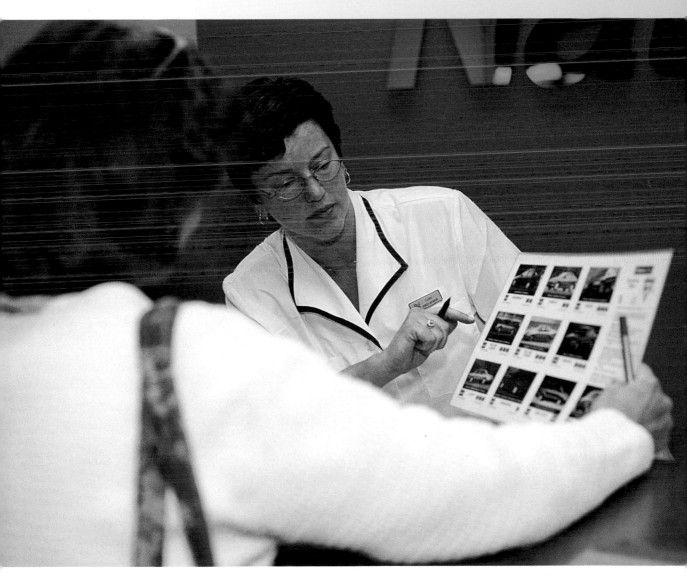

Glossary

aircraft vehicle that flies; airplanes, helicopters, gliders, and jets are different kinds of aircraft

board to get on an airplane

certified able to do a job after passing a test

communication passing information from one person to another

community area where people live, work, and shop

degree rank that a college gives a student who has finished his or her studies

deplane to get off an airplane

employee person who works for someone and is paid to do so

enclosed covered on all sides

equipment tools and machines used for a special purpose

executive someone who is in charge of an organization or a business

flight plan map and directions that tell where a plane will go

fuel something used as a source of energy, such as gasoline, oil, coal, or natural gas

government people who make the laws of a country, state, or town

mayor leader of a town or city

radar machine used to locate objects by sending out radio waves and receiving the reflected waves (radar stands for RAdio Detecting And Ranging)

reserve to arrange for something to be kept for later use

service way of providing help to a person or object

More Books to Read

Cooper, Jason. *Airports.* Vero Beach, Fla.: Rourke Corporation, 1992.

Kallen, Stuart A. *The Airport.* Edina, Minn.: ABDO and Daughters, 1997.

Miller, Marilyn. *Behind the Scenes at the Airport.* Austin, Tex.: Raintree Steck-Vaughn, 1996.

Richardson, Joy. *Airports.* New York: Franklin Watts, 1994.

Ziegler, Sandra. *A Visit to the Airport.* Chicago: Children's Press, 1988.

Index